KALTOONS

A COLLECTION OF POLITICAL CARTOONS FROM

LIGHT · FOR · ALL

THE BALTIMORE SUN

BY KEVIN KALLAUGHER

FOREWORD BY MICHAEL KINSLEY

INTRODUCTION BY JOSEPH R. L. STERNE

EDITED BY RICHARD SAMUEL WEST

To BoBwisberg
all The
Best.
KAL 96

Chatsworth Press Baltimore 1992

Chatsworth Press
29 Chatsworth Avenue
Glyndon, MD 21071

ISBN 0-9634012-0-3

Book design by Aurobind Patel

The author thanks the publisher Michael Davies,
the Marketing department of *The Baltimore Sun*,
Rich West, Joe Sterne, Mike Kinsley, Mac Naclas,
Ted Wedel, Thomas Samsel III, Sue McKeown,
Amy and Daniel Kallaugher for their invaluable
assistance and eternal patience.

Printed by Doyle Printing

Contents

To Sue, Amy, and Danny

FOREWORD by

MICHAEL KINSLEY
Senior Editor
The New Republic

KEVIN KALLAUGHER and I met almost two decades ago, when he was an undergraduate at Harvard and I was a resident adviser (pre-law!) in his dormitory, known with Ivy grandeur as Kirkland House. Kirkland House had a justified reputation as a rowdy, jockish sort of place (the students, not the staff), and I certainly never suspected that we had a world-class artist among us.

Upon graduation, KAL (as he was known even back then) went to England to play basketball–presumably because his modest height was less of a disadvantage–and to try his hand at cartooning. I lost track of his whereabouts until a few years later I saw caricatures in *The Economist* that looked remarkably like KAL's handiwork. "It can't be," I thought. But it was.

Americans prize *The Economist* as an authentic British experience, little realizing that to the British it is an export item–like Crabtree & Evelyn soap. *The Economist* sells far more copies each week in America than in Britain, and I'm sure many of those subscribers especially treasure what they suppose is the uniquely British wit of KAL's cartoons. Ironically, this American is now *The Economist's* leading illustrator and frequent cover artist.

In 1988 and 1989 I worked for *The Economist*, as editor of the American Survey section, and had the pleasure of plotting some of KAL's weekly mischief with him. But the plotting had to be done long-distance because he had recently returned to America to become the editorial cartoonist of *The Baltimore Sun*. The drawings in this book are all from the pages of that newspaper. KAL's career has flowered at *The Sun* and he is now widely syndicated as well. It is terribly ungrateful of him to include in this book a savage portrayal of *The Sun's* most famous contributor–H.L. Mencken–as a sacred cow.

But then ruthless savagery is the meat and potatoes (sp?) of political cartoonist. They have license to say things in their art that mere scribblers are forbidden to say in words. For example, the editor-in-chief of *The New Republic*, where I work, has a rule (enforced erratically) against describing people as animals. He says it dehumanizing and reminiscent of Communist propaganda, which was always labeling enemies as "braying hyenas" and whatnot. And perhaps it is.

And yet the pages of this book are a veritable zoo, and not just filled with donkeys and elephants. There are copious snakes and dragons, sharks and various other marine life, rats and Saddam Hussein–hilariously–as a self satisfied camel. And then there are the rabbits. In the summer of 1992, Ross Perot famously compared George Bush to a rabbit, but KAL beat him to it in May 1991 (see page 57). And for good measure, in March '92, he did Bill Clinton as a rabbit as well–outsmarting Paul Tsongas as Elmer Fudd.

There are many hilarious drawings and great jokes here, jovial reminders of the follies of the past few years–in Baltimore and Maryland as well as in America and the world. (Really though, KAL is Donald Schaefer ALWAYS a clown?) But there are also serious moments that are poignant and even profound. See, for example, the Ayatollah Khomeini arriving in hell on page 88.

I can't remember whether, as pre-law adviser in Kirkland House, I ever gave KAL and actual advice. I'd like to think I advised him not to become a lawyer and to pursue his art. "A brilliant future awaits you," I might have said. At any rate, that's my story from now on.

INTRODUCTION by

JOE STERN
Editor
The Baltimore Sun

"GIVE ME A GOOD CARTOONIST," H. L. Mencken once declared, "and I can fire half the editorial staff." Mencken would know. He was a contemporary of *The Baltimore Sun*'s Edmund Duffy, three times a Pulitizer Prize winner, whose savage drawings of the likes of Hitler, Mussolini and Stalin capture forever the frightening era when dictatorship stalked the globe.

There was nothing funny about Duffy. His cartoons were bleak, unrelenting examples of the slash and bash school whose enduring influence can still be seen in the cartoons of the *Washington Post*'s Herblock.

The Baltimore Sun gloried in Duffy, for good cause. Yet when it came time to change, the newspaper turned to his almost exact opposite, another legendary cartoonist by the name of Richard Q. "Moco" Yardley. Whereas Duffy was spare and natty, Yardley was a big, smiling, rolly-polly guy whose cartoons, no matter how serious the subject or the message, were full of whimsy, sunshine, good humor. He captured the essence of "Bawlmer"–its crab cakes, its "One-sixth" political bosses, its good life on Chesapeake Bay.

Neil A. Grauer, a Baltimore-based student of the cartoonist's art, once observed that while "Victims of Duffy's bludgeons often wanted to shoot him, the politicians ridiculed by Yardley's pen (and make no mistake, he made them look like idiots) begged for the original drawings."

After Yardley, in 1972, came the inimitable Tom Flannery, who in just a few lean strokes of the pen could skewer his subjects with dark yet gentle irony. His was an understated talent, whose work anticipated the elaborate and extraordinary art contained in this book.

How Kevin Kallaugher came to grace the pages of *The Baltimore Sun* is worth recounting, at least to me, because his hiring was the single most important service I have rendered my newspaper in almost 40 years on the payroll. The tale begins in the summer of 1987. Rumors had been about in the tiny cartoon fraternity that Tom Flannery was contemplating retirement. Week after week, unsolicited portfolios would come over the transom from artists eager for a shot at the Duffy-Yardley-Flannery succession. And week after week, they would be wearily rejected by an editor bracing for a nationwide search.

Then, one day, a packet arrived from England. I remember the moment. I opened it, preparing to give it the usual treatment, when I gasped–literally gasped–at what lay before me. Here was art. Here was a journalist's eye for outrage one moment, rollicking humor the next. Here was Kevin Kallaugher, whose work under the name of KAL I had seen often enough in that great British weekly, *The Economist*.

I resolved on the instant to bring him to Baltimore and, lucky for me, I had a publisher in Reg Murphy who agreed. Kevin Kallaugher, it seemed to me, was a cartoonist who had something of Duffy's impact, Yardley's whimsy and Flannery's deftness plus his own outlook and precision of line. He was clearly destined for *The Sun*, which would give him the freedom and the platform to develop into a leading political cartoonist.

KAL's first cartoon appeared in *The Sun* in December 1988. It showed President-elect George Bush emerging triumphantly from a football huddle in which a hapless Ronald Reagan is getting piled on by Irangate, drugs, the Middle East and especially the deficit. The original hangs in my office, a treasure.

Kevin works just down the hall, in an office he shares with a seven foot papier-mache figure of his version of George Bush. Often, he can be found staring out the window or meticulously peering through a magnifying glass to put in a hairline stroke. Just as often, he can be seen wandering around the building to chat with or bounce ideas off of reporters and janitors. He does not suffer much editorial supervision, and he does not get it. When you have a genius on the premises, you don't mess with him.

The following pages prove the point. KAL's political statements weather well. His perspective is never askew. His variety of style and approach is forever fresh. He is KAL of *The Baltimore Sun*.

THE VISION THING

December 4 1988

January 25 1989

May 20 1990

June 28 1990

July 19 1990

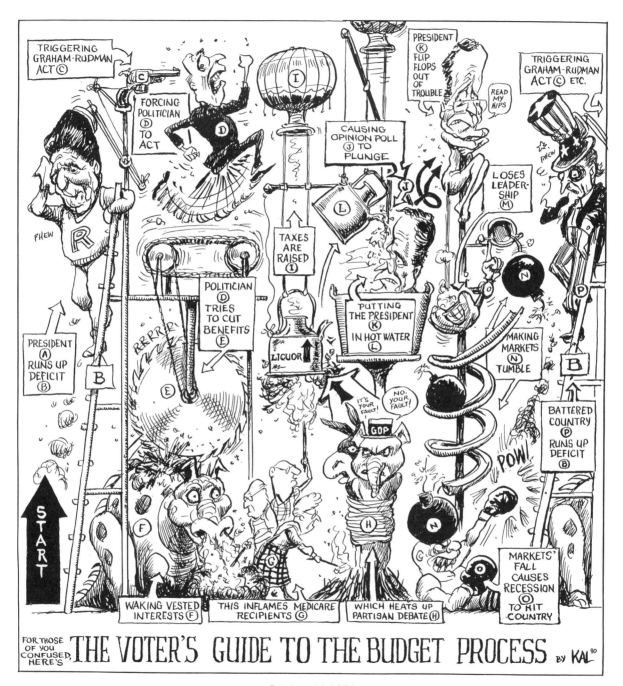

THE VOTER'S GUIDE TO THE BUDGET PROCESS

November 17 1990

July 3 1989

June 24 1990

June 7 1991

April 7 1989

February 2 1989

April 19 1991

March 11 1990

KAL '89 BALTIMORE SUN

August 31 1989

September 3 1989

April 10 1992

January 3 1990

September 22 1991

February 28 1992

May 16 1991

February 6 1992

March 29 1992

May 17 1992

September 15 1989

February 5 1992

ALL THESE SCIENTISTS DO IS COMPLAIN ABOUT THE OZONE LAYER.
LOOK OUT THERE, SMITHSON. DO YOU SEE A HOLE?

May 31 1992

April 22 1990

THE NATION DISCUSSES ABORTION

May 1 1989

December 22 1988

September 16 1990

September 10 1991

October 15 1991

August 13 1991

IMPORTANT NEWS YOU SHOULD KNOW:
THE SUPREME COURT IS PASSING THE DELICATE ISSUES OF ABORTION AND EUTHANASIA TO THE STATE LEGISLATURES

OTHER IMPORTANT NEWS YOU SHOULD KNOW:

February 7 1991

"BAD NEWS...
THERE'S BEEN ANOTHER MERGER"

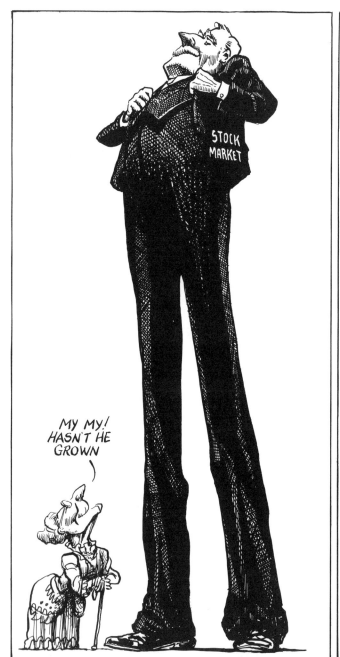

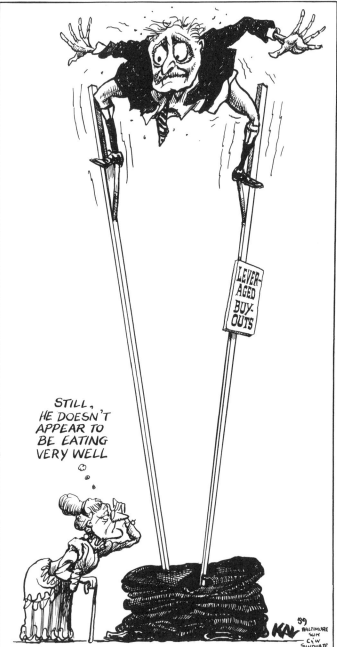

October 18 1989

October 17 1989

November 3 1989

July 5 1992

February 27 1992

April 4 1991

April 21 1991

May 8 1991

May 1 1992

May 5 1992

May 13 1992

May 15 1992

May 8 1992

March 18 1992

I AM
THE
CANDIDATE
OF
CHANGE

KAL '92
BALTO.
SUN
CW SYN.

July 21 1992

January 26 1992

February 25 1992

March 20 1992

April 14 1992

May 14 1992

KAL '92
BALTO.SUN CWSYND.

July 20 1992

July 29 1992

April 16 1989

April 24 1992

BEEP
BOOP
BOOP
BOOP
BEEP
BOOP
BEEP

HELLO?

WELCOME TO THE U.S. GOVERNMENT BLAME LINE!
TO BLAME SOMEONE FOR THE S&L CRISIS - PRESS ONE
TO BLAME SOMEONE FOR THE GULF CRISIS - PRESS TWO
TO BLAME SOMEONE FOR THE BUDGET CRISIS PRESS THREE...

BEEP!

WELCOME TO THE S&L CRISIS BLAME LINE!
TO BLAME CORRUPT POLITICIANS PRESS ONE
TO BLAME GREEDY EXECUTIVES PRESS TWO
TO BLAME RONALD REAGAN PRESS THREE...

BEEP!

WELCOME TO THE CORRUPT POLITICIAN BLAME LINE!
TO BLAME THE CAMPAIGN FINANCE SYSTEM - PRESS ONE
TO BLAME AN INDIVIDUAL POLITICIAN - PRESS TWO...

BEEP!

HELLO, MAY I HELP YOU?

HELLO! A PERSON! FINALLY!
I'M A TAXPAYER AND I CAN'T SEEM TO FIND ANYONE TO BLAME FOR THIS $500,000,000,000 BILL I HAVE TO PAY

JUST CONNECTING YOU...

THANKS!

BILL
YOU ARE STUCK WITH PAYING THE FOLLOWING OBSCENE AMOUNT...

WELCOME TO THE U.S. GOVERNMENT BLAME LINE!
TO BLAME SOMEONE FOR THE S&L CRISIS PRESS ONE
TO BLAME SOMEONE FOR THE GULF CRISIS PRESS TWO...

BILL

KAL '90 BALTIMORE SUN C.W.N. SYNDICATE

December 16 1990

THE NEW WORLD ORDER

February 17 1991

July 7 1989

May 24 1990

June 7 1989

March 30 1990

August 19 1990

August 29 1990

October 17 1990

August 30 1990

December 2 1990

January 20 1991

January 23 1991

February 12 1991

February 15 1991

February 24 1991

March 5 1991

March 6 1991

March 22 1991

June 9 1991

August 4 1991

April 16 1991

April 28 1991

July 23 1991

August 7 1991

December 5 1991

September 6 1989

October 12 1989

March 15 1992

March 19 1992

May 29 1991

AFGHANISTAN

February 14 1989

August 15 1989

THE EVOLUTION OF THE IRON LADY

1979 1980 1981 1982 1983 1986 1987 1988 1989 1990

KAL '90 BALTIMORE SUN C-N SYNDICATE

November 27 1990

117

January 12 1992

January 5 1992

April 8 1990

THE
RED BLUES

July 11 1989

December 7 1988

March 29 1990

RED CHINA

KAL '89
BALTIMORE
SUN

June 6 1989

January 25 1990

October 8 1989

February 11 1990

April 23 1991

February 6 1990

August 30 1989

August 1 1991

August 2 1991

July 8 1990

June 20 1991

October 16 1990

August 23 1991

December 10 1991

December 12 1991

December 26 1991

March 26 1992

July 3 1990

December 6 1989

BAWLMER
AND BEYOND

February 8 1991

May 3 1991

March 13 1991

February 20 1990

155

October 2 1991

November 4 1990

August 18 1989

July 19 1991

December 19 1989

March 24 1991

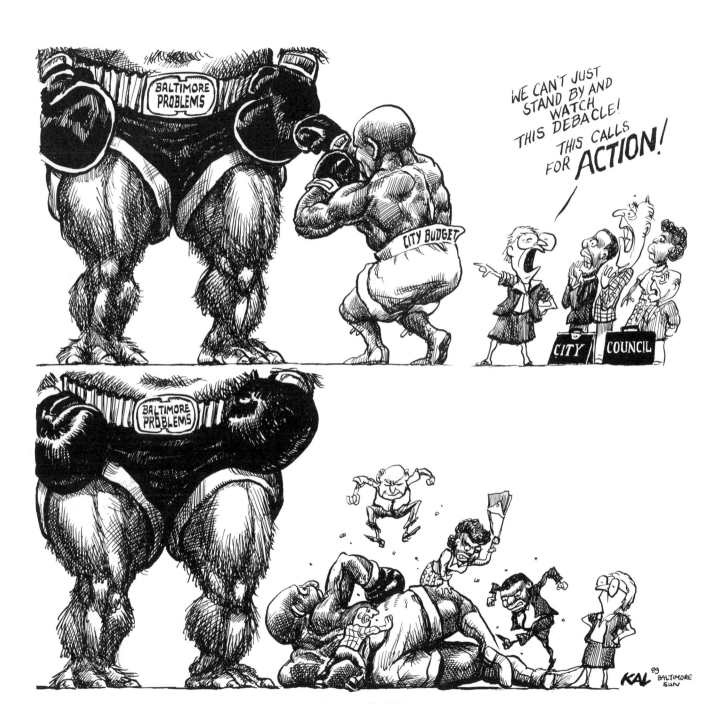

THE PROBLEM IN CHOOSING SOMEONE TO FILL DR. HUNTER'S SHOES

The bench reads: BALTIMORE / THE CITY THAT READS

Signed: KAL '90 BALTIMORE SUN

May 11 1990

January 21 1990

March 1 1990

December 7 1989

May 15 1991

October 6 1991

September 20 1991

October 18 1991

THE STREETS OF **GOTHAM CITY** WERE A DANGEROUS JUNGLE WITH A VILLAIN AROUND EVERY CORNER

ROBBERS CROOKS AND CRIMINALS WERE EVERYWHERE

ALL AFTER YOUR MONEY

KAL 89 BALTIMORE SUN

BUT THERE WAS ONE VILLAIN WHOSE CUNNING KNEW NO BOUNDS. IN ONE WEEK HE TOOK **MILLIONS OF DOLLARS** FROM INNOCENT CITIZENS. WHO WAS THIS **DASTARDLY DEMON?** WAS IT THE JOKER? WAS IT THE RIDDLER? **NO!** IT WAS...

THE MERCHANDIZER ©

GET YOUR OFFICIAL BATMAN T-SHIRTS, RINGS, AND UNDERWEAR HERE! BATMAN WATCHES! BATMAN PERFUME, HAIRGEL, AND NAILCLIPPER! BATGUNS! BATBALLS! BATBATS! ALL THINGS BATTY HERE!

BATMAN FAN

$13.00

BUTTONS

MERCHANDIZER DOLLS SOLD SEPARATELY

June 29 1989

May 29 1992

September 5 1990

March 7 1990

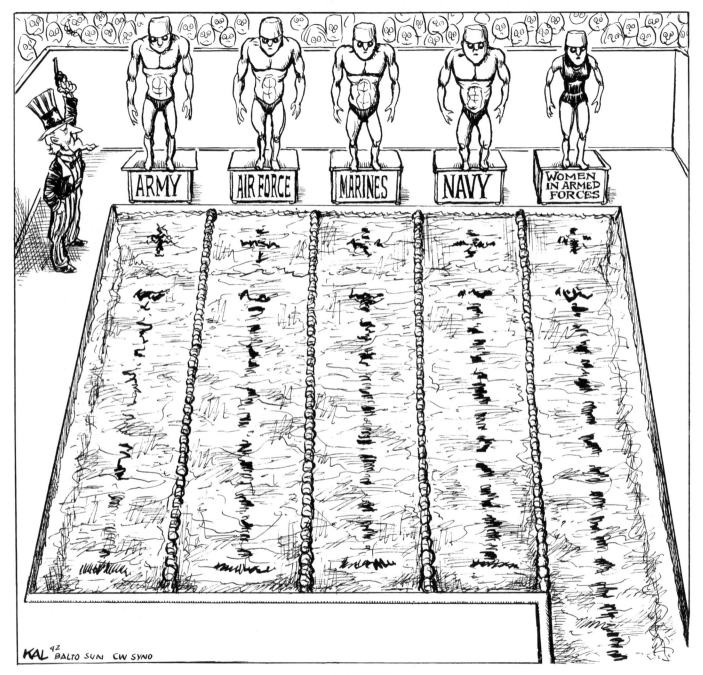

August 2 1992

AMERICAN ART
LURCHES FORWARD
INTO THE
17TH CENTURY

October 5 1990

December 15 1991